About the Author

VALERIE JEANNIS is a youth motivational speaker and life coach on a mission to inspire young women and youth around the world to say yes to their lives and to live out their dreams and potentials.

Unashamed to use her life as a teaching mechanism, Valerie's REAL Talk and in your face messages inspires communities to believe and invest in themselves and to just go for it.

To learn more about Valerie' keynotes, workshops and programs, visit www.ValerieJeannis.com

Valerie Jeannis

Founder of League of Extraordinary Young Women

Valerie Jeannis

Changing the Way You See Yourself

Valerie Jeannis

I AM BEAUTIFUL

I AM BEAUTIFUL Copyright 2012 by Valerie Jeannis

All rights reserved. No part of this book may be used or reproduced in any manner whatsoever without written permission from Valerie Jeannis, except as provided by the United States of America copyright law or in the case of brief quotations embodied in articles and reviews. The scanning, uploading and distribution of this book via the Internet or via any other means without the permission of the publisher is illegal and punishable by law.

Please purchase only authorized electronic editions and do not participate in or encourage electronic piracy of copyrighted materials. Your support of the author's rights is sincerely appreciated.

Printed in the United States of America

First Printing: 2012

* In order to protect the identity of certain individuals pseudonyms have been used.

* All scripture references were taken from the King James Version of the Bible

Valerie Jeannis

I AM BEAUTIFUL

To those who feel disqualified because of their past,
You are not too bad.
You are not too far gone.
You are not too messed up.

Simply as you are, you are chosen.
Simply as you are, you are more than enough.

Simply as you are, *you are beautiful.*

Valerie Jeannis

Table of Contents

Acknowledgements
Share with Us
Song of Myself
(Forward).

1. I Am Not My Past
2. I Am Able
3. I Am Whole
4. I Am Beautiful
5. I Am Loved
6. I Am Forgiven
7. I Am Worth It
8. I Am Grateful
9. I Am Alive
10. I Am Moving Forward
11. I Am Somebody
12. I Am Powerful
13. I Am Extraordinary

A Special Message
Real Talk Presentations
I Am Beautiful Academy
I Am a Super Role Model Leadership Program

Valerie Jeannis

x

Acknowledgements

It's been said that behind every great man is a great woman. Well behind every dream realized and every vision fulfilled is a group of people who in one way or another fueled the dreamer and the vision. I am so grateful for every single person who came along on my journey and contributed to who I am and where I am today.

To my Lord and Savior Jesus Christ, who taught me who I was through His unchanging Word, thank you for choosing me and freeing me to be the best me and to live my best life now. Thank you for continuing to do exceedingly and abundantly above all that I could ask or think. Thank you for being more than God, thank you for being my Friend who sticks closer than a brother and who loves me at all times without exception.

To my mom, words are not enough. Mom, you are to me what only you can be. You gave me room to pursue my dream, which meant everything and made the difference. You stuck by me and always reassured me that all things are possible through Christ. I thank you so much and I love you so much more.

To my family, thank you for believing when it was only an idea and for bragging before I even had anything to show.

To my Bishop, Bishop Carlton T. Brown of Bethel Gospel Assembly, thank you for always finding time to thoroughly respond to my numerous emails filled with questions and for meeting, counseling and sharing with me in spite of your crazy busy schedule.

To Dr. Rev. Andrew Omotoso, thank you for always encouraging me to be myself fully with no apology and no compromise. Thank you for being a model of a bold and faithful man of God.

To Saundra A. Heath, my friend and mentor, thank you for listening to me and allowing me to be me. Thank you for always speaking to the possibilities with honestly and enthusiasm.

To Elder Wendie Trott who heard the vision and said it was possible, thank you for believing in me when it was just an idea on paper and for always saying yes it's possible, especially when I wasn't sure if it was going to happen. Not only did you say you believe in me, but you backed it up with your support and services as an editor. Thank you for making sure that every comma and colon was in place.

To Ifetaya Burlow, thank you for being my friend and prayer partner and incredible source of support.

To my Nana Joan Byrd, thank you for spending countless hours in the winter cold listening to me share for as long as I needed to. (When she sensed that I was done, she would say "I love you, now leave me alone, I'm going home.")

Katie Cavanaugh, my friend and coach, your faith in me and encouragement fueled me as I embarked on this journey. Thank you for never giving up on me, for constantly encouraging me, and always greeting me with such excitement and enthusiasm.

To Ann McIndoo, my author's coach, thank you for being an eagle on my journey and for showing me that it was possible to be an author today. To Mishael, Ann's incredible support team, thank you for making sure that I had all the information and tools I needed to get started on this incredible journey

To Richard Krawczek, an unexpected friend who complimented my shoes, thank you for being available and answering my questions and for not only listening to the vision, but for giving it a name that embodied the goal, League of Extraordinary Young Women.

Valerie Jeannis

Share with Us

I would love to hear what you think. Please let me know how this book affected you and what your take aways were.

Also please send me any stories, poems or cartoons that you would like to share.

Send these stories to:

I Am Beautiful Movement
Valerie Jeannis
55 West 116th Street
Suite 360
New York, NY 10026

Email for stories: Hello@ValerieJeannis
Email for letters: Info@ValerieJeannis.cm
Website: www.ValerieJeannis.com

I hope you enjoy reading this book as much as I enjoyed writing it. It has truly been a labor of love.

Valerie Jeannis

I AM BEAUTIFUL

Song of Myself

When I stepped out into the distended world
It was as though I was looking into the uncelebrated,
    unrenowned mirror of me

In it I saw...
The homeless guy sleeping on the floor, not out of
    sleepiness, but out of sheer discouragement in life and
    in the seemingly high-hat, unaware individuals who so
    often pass by him without a second thought or pang of
    compassion
The sad weighed down individual who always gets picked
    on because no matter how much milk he drinks, he just
    can't seem to grow
The heavy-hearted girl staring into space with a look of
    Shakespearean sorrow because she lost the first love of
    her life
The world-weary, Jezebelic girl who just wants to be
    accepted

I saw...
The masked individual who forcefully and vigorously laughs
    at every joke out of fear that if she stops someone just
    might laugh at her
The pregnant, middle-aged woman who is dejected
    because after all this time she still can't seem to get it
    right
The teenage couple, expecting their first child,
    contemplating how this could have happened after
    only fifteen minutes

The group of girls who are continuously laughing, gossiping, and talking loud, afraid that if they are silent long enough, the torments of their souls might cause them to break down in tears
The evidently once so beautiful woman who now puts on much too much make-up in an unsuccessful attempt to conceal the price she pays for blindly loving a man

I saw...
The sick boy wondering, "If there is a God how come I'm dying?"
The mother wondering "Where's God, and why isn't He answering our prayers or listening to my baby's crying?"
The girl enviously looking at the person across from her, putting herself down and wishfully praying for a beauty so perfect, with the misconstrued notion that it'll be the answer to all her prayers
The goddess whose immaculate grandeur, which is so often seen as a blessing, struggling under the pressure of what she finds to be her most prominent curse

I saw...
The troubled teen whose cries for help fall on deaf ears
The girl who gets frightened by her reflection, because for a brief moment she forgets that under all the make-up, without the contacts, fake hair, fake eyelashes, fake beauty mark, the piercings, tattoos, and the "in" clothes, it's just her
The one lying in the hospital because, since she didn't look like that beautiful actress, life just wasn't worth living

The scorned teen mother glaring at her newborn, the product of her mirage of love and constant reminder of her stupidity
The teenage girl filled with a sense of despondence because she lost her virginity, and she can't even remember his name

I saw...
The innocent girl so drowned by the sorrows of the circumstances of life that she's not even conscious of the tears streaming down her face
The desperate mother seeking help because her child has become a stranger
The old lady searching the eyes of the pedestrians in silent prayer for a seat, and the faces that looked back in denial to her prayer with the exception of that one youthful ear pierced, hair braided, baggy pants wearing "outcast" of society who offered his seat
The disheartened guy wondering about the child he would never know because she got an abortion and then told him

I saw...
The young evangelist cutting with the double-edged sword and offering healing for those with open wounds
The fourteen year-old on trial because he wanted to show his friend that he was cool but killed him with the gun instead
The baby who has to die because "it's just a mass of blood" and no one can hear its cry
The girl who was offered a rose for her beauty just as she was wondering will she ever find love in this lifetime

Valerie Jeannis

The frustrated and discouraged young man who was denied another job because of the mistakes of his past

I saw...
The daughter who walks by unnoticed by her mother, who just never had enough time, right into the arms of death
The bride-to-be, who once told her best friend that dads are just good for money, crying because now that her dad is gone, who's going to walk her down the aisle
The one who is finally able to breathe because Jesus washed away all her sins
The lost soul whose search for love left her with five kids at the age of 20 and a heart broken seemingly beyond repair

I saw...
The disheveled young woman sharing her story, singing her song, and asking for some change to get by
The angel preaching a message of hope and love and forgiveness and happiness, a message that seems like a chimera compared to reality, so therefore falls on ears too scarred by the veracity of life
The joyous little girl whose smile radiates the sun in the heart of all those she encounters, because no one can understand how an orphan child with nothing to call her own, who goes without eating days at a time, can be so full of celestial peace
The desperate girl who constantly has sex for the sake of "love" because that's the only way they'll stay
The confused seven year-old boy who is too young to know what sexual abuse is but old enough to understand that something very bad just happened to him

I AM BEAUTIFUL

I saw...
The stranger who exchanged a smile with the young
    student giving her hope that she is going to make it
The lawyer, the two nurses, the pediatrician, the teacher,
    the social worker, the youth director, the group of
    friends who grew up together, celebrating 'cause they
    made it,
The broken little one who found out too early that life
    doesn't consist of fairy tales and happy endings, just a
    lot of liars
The benevolent God saying "I am here my child just
    welcome Me, and I will come"

See all these are part of me
The me I was, the me I hope never to be

So when I say that I'm looking into the mirror of me
It's not the me people so quickly see
It's the me of past, the me of present,
The me of what if, the me of never
The Song of Myself is the Mirror of Me

The Song of Myself
Valerie Jeannis © 2007

Valerie Jeannis

(*forward*).

Once you know who you are, you know that anything is beyond possible for you. - Valerie Jeannis

No one would have ever said looking at me in my preteen years, now there goes a future author. Instead, one lady walked up to me when I was 14 and whispered in my ears "You are going to get pregnant by the time you're 16. Trick." I didn't even know what that word meant, but that didn't stop it from becoming my identity.

> *"Look at man the way he is and he only becomes worse; look at him for the way he could be, and then he will become what he should be."* Goethe

For a long time, I allowed the misconceptions and opinions of others to define me and what was possible for my life. But I am so glad for transformation. I am so grateful for the day that I found out that I was created, loved and forgiven and that I was fearfully and wonderfully made. Learning who I was freed me from the labels and judgments of people who thought they knew me. Not only was I more than they knew, turns out, I was more than I knew.

As I changed the way I saw myself, I realized that I truly was free: free to start over, free to be who and all I was intended to be, free to live and free to pursue my dreams, even the ones I hadn't even dreamed yet.

I Am Beautiful started out as one girl's journey to self-discovery and turned into a movement to let every young woman and woman know she is beautiful, she is more than her past and she was created for a purpose. And here's the great thing: as you change the way you see yourself, you will awaken to the possibilities that are available to you. You will also know that everything is beyond possible for you. It is possible... it is possible to live a life beyond your current circumstances. It is possible to make a new choice. It is possible to decide who you want to be and what you want from your life. It is possible to dare to dream big and to pursue your dreams and for your dreams to become a reality.

"You are more beautiful than you know
More talented than you think
& More loved than you can imagine" – Unknown

As you read the pages of this book, I encourage you to keep a journal and reflect about your own life. Stay in touch by visiting www.IAmBeautifulMovement.com and join the movement.

I Am *Not My Past*

As I looked out the window of the M3 bus, I didn't see or hear anything. I don't even remember whether or not I was crying. I was broken, shocked and angry.

I remember telling God that if this is what sex was, then I don't care anymore.

Forget waiting till I am married.

I give up.

> Have you ever had a moment where you did something and looked back and asked yourself, what were you thinking?

All these different thoughts kept running through my mind.

"How could this have happened Valerie?

How do you leave your mom in bed - SICK - to go to some guy's house who you don't even know?

Valerie!!! What happened?!"

I even remember the lie I told my mom when she asked me where I was going. I had a prepaid phone at the time which I bought in the Bronx, so I told her that I had to go back to the same store to buy a refill card.

She knew I was lying too, but she was sick with the flu and didn't have the strength to fight with me.

So I left, got in a taxi and rushed over to his house.

> *Have you ever had a moment where you did something and looked back and asked yourself, what were you thinking?*

This was one of those moments.

Why did I go over there in the first place? I don't know. Why did I get into the taxi? I don't know. But yet, there I was.

There was someone else in the house, so I wasn't worried. After all, this was the same guy I went to the movies with a few days ago who, when I leaned in during one of those "perfect kiss moments", he leaned back and said, "No, I respect you too much."

Besides, it wasn't the first time I put myself in a compromising situation.

I even went to meet some guy I met online and took my friend with me putting us both in a bad situation. Turned out this guy was a drug dealer who lived in a basement, slept with a gun under his pillow "just in case," and had his door rigged so that the only way you could get out was if he let you out.

Thank God because nothing happened to either one of us.

When you constantly put yourself in these bad situations and "get away with it," you start to feel invincible.

Well that was then, and this was now.

How could someone act so nice in one instance and turn out to be a totally different person?

Everything started out fine. We went to his room, watched TV and just talked. Within an hour, I found myself on the floor with a guy I didn't really know and NEVER even kissed on top of me. All I could do was just lay there paralyzed for what had to be the longest 60 seconds of my life. I couldn't stop crying and saying, "No! No! No!" Then all of a sudden he stopped and said, "Come on, let's go."

There is something inside of you that seems to break when you find yourself in the last place you ever expected.

There is something inside of you that seems to break when you find yourself in the last place you ever expected. It feels like certain things don't matter anymore, as though something has died. At that point, the only thing going through my mind was, *if people thought I was bad before, just wait*. I was 16; going on 17, with my mind made up to just go crazy. I would have done it too, if it wasn't for that speaker and if Manny hadn't come into my life.

The Revival

Not too long after "the incident" there was a youth revival at my church, where a young preacher came and spoke about how no matter what you have done, you are never too bad for God. He spoke about love, acceptance and belonging which, above everything, was what I wanted: to be loved simply for who I was and in spite of what I'd done or could ever do. That was the beginning of my love relationship with Jesus. That's when I became a Christian. Please remind me to write about my experiences in an Emotional Healing Support Group and being introduced to the work of Joyce Meyer.

A few weeks later, I was sitting in the back of the church talking with a group of my friends when Manny made his entrance. Everyone was so surprised to see him because he hadn't been to church in years. Plus we all heard that he joined a gang and left home.

He quickly got an audience when he started sharing his story about life on the streets, joining a gang, going to prison and how God turned it all around. As I was sitting there listening to him, I remember thinking, *Well, if God can do it for him, He can do it for me too. I'm not that bad.*

That Was a Mistake

I was so excited about the possibility of change that I asked Manny to do a Bible Study with me. That was Mistake #1. I should have found a woman to ask for help. That would have been the wise choice. And I should have listened to my mom when she warned me and said, "Valerie don't do it." Thinking I knew better, I dismissed her advice.

Not long after we started Bible Study, Manny declared that "God showed me who you are going to be with." I was so excited because God was talking about me!!! So after I named every single guy in that church, he finally told me that it was him. I was a little taken aback, but I really wanted to do things right, so if God said it, then I would do it. The only problem was that, at the time, I didn't think God could or would speak to me, so every time Manny said "God said," I believed him. That was Mistake #2: thinking that God couldn't speak to me directly.

Rather than question Manny, my response was "If God gives you something; He is not going to take it away, is He?" Manny, of course, said, "No." So I replied, "Well, that means we are going to be together forever, right?" "Yes." And that was the beginning of a 4 ½ year relationship which almost cost me my life. Who you choose to let into your life can literally alter the course of your life.

> Who you choose to let into your life can literally alter the course of your life.

Things started off fine, but then quickly changed. Looking back there were so many signs that he was not the person I was supposed to be with or that he was not who he claimed to be; nevertheless I stayed. When I asked if we could 'take a break,' he said that there were no breaks. I should never have asked his permission to leave. I should have just left. Shoulda, coulda, woulda, but I didn't.

That Was a Sign

It was about 2 weeks into the relationship when he said, "I love you." I didn't feel the same way and I didn't want to lie, so I just didn't say anything. The first time he let it slide, but the second time he said it, and I said nothing, he bullied me into responding that I loved him in return. That was a sign.

About two months into the relationship, Manny needed a suit for a special event, but he didn't have the money. I wasn't too crazy about his taste in clothes, so I took birthday money, which I had saved up, and "borrowed" additional money from my mom and gave it to Manny.

When I did, he said, "I am gonna marry you! I would do it now if I could." That was another sign. The fact that he chose that particular moment to make that declaration was telling, but I didn't know it at the time, so I was all smiles. *Marry ME???* I felt so special. When he told me he was going to pay me back, in my naiveté I responded, "No, no that's ok. Since we're going to get married, what's mine is yours and what's yours is mine." That was stupid, because from that point on, it was pretty much always mine becoming his. I was always the one who ended up paying, which didn't feel good at all.

Not too long after that, he came to pick me up so we could hang out, and as I walking towards him, a guy on the street made an inappropriate comment. Knowing it was nothing serious; I just smiled and kept on walking. Manny was standing on the corner and when he saw me smile, he got so mad that right there in the middle of the street he started yelling at me, and punched a car THAT WAS NOT EVEN HIS!!!!, which set off the car alarm and triggered the other alarms to go off as well. I was so embarrassed and shocked. I just stood there getting yelled at. That too was a sign.

I don't remember how that conversation ended, but I stayed. After that happened, I just stopped smiling at people in public, especially guys. I use to be someone who was always smiling. However, it got to the point where I would call him when I got home from school and proudly report that I went the whole day without smiling at anyone. That was another sign. In the midst of the positive changes I was making (and there were positive changes), I started losing who I was and remolding myself into who he said and thought I should be.

Slowly but surely, I started isolating myself, ending friendships and pushing everyone away, including my mom, until he was my only friend. My world revolved around him, God, church and school.

Don't Miss Your Exit
I remember talking myself and several of my cousins to go on this roller coaster ride, which I usually avoid at all costs, and on top of that I decided that we should sit in the very front. The whole time we are standing online, I just didn't want to do this. And as the worker is making sure that we were all sitting down I called him over and told him that I didn't want to do it, and he asked me if I wanted to get off. I hesitated and he was like ok and just walked away. As soon as the roller coaster started inching forward, I knew I

to let me off, but it was too late. I missed the opportunity to make an exit before the ride started.

All those signs were exits that I missed. Each of them made it clear that Manny was not the person I should have been with, but unfortunately like many women (young and old); I made excuses for him, rationalized his behavior and stayed.

Based on my experiences and the many conversations that I had with others, after about 3 months in a relationship, most people know whether or not they should continue with the relationship. But for whatever reason, too many don't trust their "intuition", miss their exit and end up staying. The thing is, when you miss your exit, it takes longer and makes it harder to leave.

> The thing is, when you miss your exit, it takes longer and makes it harder to leave.

Don't miss your exit.

I Am *Able*

I change my mind, because I can. - Valerie Jeannis

ঙ‍ও

Every single one of us has the right and the ability to change our minds. It took a while, but started changing my mind.

About 3 years into the relationship even though he didn't officially propose, we were planning the wedding. Then one Friday night as we sat in an empty diner in the 42nd street terminal, he proposed and I said yes. No fuss, no grand romantic gesture...nothing. Now there's a story I loved sharing every time people asked, smh.

A Semi-Fool

I am no fool. I know that I don't always get things right and that there are things that can always be done better, that's why I am open to correction and constructive criticism. But it wasn't always that way. There was a time that I thought that I knew best and that I had all the answers.

As I was getting ready for the wedding, it was clear to everyone except for me that I was making a mistake. It was years after the break up when people stated telling me "yeah, here's what was really going on." I was floored because these were the same people who were part of the bridal party. They were going to just let me go through with it and be witnesses as I signed my life away. When I asked why they never said anything, they said it was because they didn't know how I was going to respond and there were afraid that I would go back and tell my then "fiancé" because of how I responded to people and correction in the past.

Let's face it, when you correct someone, you never know how they will respond. Either they will thank you and really appreciate it or make you an enemy. That fear has led many people to forever hold their peace. But it is a risk worth taking, because had someone not been bold enough to come up to me and say four simple life changing words, I could have been unhappily married right now.

> *When you correct someone, you never know how they will responds.*

"Separation Is Not Divorce"

The closer I got to the wedding, the more doubts I started having because of the things that I was noticing Manny. One Sunday after church I was walking across the street when one of the leaders came up to me and said "Separation is not divorce." That's it. No explanation. Nothing. Just, "separation is not divorce." And for whatever reason that made sense to me and it was like an answer to my prayers.

Not too long after that I told Manny that I wanted out. The first time I told him, he said that he gave and that he was going back to his old life in the streets. I did not want to be the reason he went back, so I said, "Fine, I'll stay."

I Am Letting Go

Too many times we hold on when we should let go, even when holding on means killing some part of ourselves.

Holding on when you should have let go sometimes means losing so much more and it can mean losing yourself.

As I was deciding whether or not to end my engagement and cancel all the wedding plans. There were so many things that went through my mind. I didn't want people to talk about me and I was afraid of what they would think. I didn't want to be single again and have to go through the dating process again. I didn't want to lose all the down payments. I didn't want to be the reason he gave up and went back to the life he left behind.

In life you have to learn when to let go and cut your losses, because holding on when you should have let go sometimes means losing so much more and it can mean losing yourself.

The Final Straw

After the first attempted breakup, I thought things would get better, but I was wrong. The final straw came when I discovered a significant amount of money was missing from my account and when I called him to ask him what happened to the money, he said, "I went shopping!" I was dumbfounded. So I asked him the next logical question that I could think of, "Well, did you get me anything?" "No."

For some reason that really irritated me because not only did you take my money without permission but didn't even get me anything!

After I got off the phone something still didn't feel right, so I called my bank and did some investigation to find out where was this money spent. As I was calling around I just started laughing because I kept thinking "this is ridiculous." I didn't want to be in a relationship where I had to play detective to find out what was really going on.

Up until that point, I never shared anything that was going on in the relationship with anyone because Manny always said I told people what was going on they would just break up. I needed someone to talk to but I didn't know who to trust. So I called the one person who was bold enough to tell me the truth – that one church leader.

When he picked up, it was as though a dam broke...I shared 4 ½ years of frustration and disappointments in about an hour. When I was done, his one advice to me was to call Manny back and make it clear where I stood.

So that's exactly what I did. I called Manny and told him that it was over. Since we were never the on again off again type, he knew that this time I was serious and he was not happy, in fact, he was livid. He told me "I am coming over right now to get all my stuff."'

Since I was home alone and my mom was out of town, I didn't want to be alone with him. He was a slim guy, but he was strong. (I saw him punch the door of a metal mailbox and then rip the door off within seconds, just because he was mad.)

Since I couldn't get anyone to come over in time, I just prayed and made sure that all his stuff was packed and by the door (what a reality check to see that 4 ½ years was able to fit into 1 box!)

He was at my house within the hour and I was greeted with a flow of curses and insults and the whole time he was yelling, I was just looking at him and thinking "oh my God, oh my God, I can't believe I did it. I can't believe I made it out. Jesus! It's really over." It took everything in me to restrain my smile.

It was finally over.

Valerie Jeannis

I Am *Whole*

"Just as I am, I Am Whole." – Valerie Jeannis

☙❦

Going through the breakup was like going through a mini divorce and when it was all said and done, I felt lost. I spent so long trying to be what Manny wanted me to be and who others thought I should be that I didn't know who I was anymore.

The journey to discovering who you are and who you want to be starts with a decision…

It's so easy to forget who you are when you spend so long being scared, pretending and trying to fit some image.

It's been said that "the journey of a 1000 miles begins with one step." Well, the journey to discovering who you are and who you want to be starts with a decision… a decision to be open to the fact that you are so much more than you know.

Still Single

From the time I was 16 until now, I've had two relationships. After my first relationship (with Manny) ended I was so sure I was ready that I didn't even want to give myself time to breathe or heal. I was just searching for the next person.

When you're in your twenties and single, one of the number one questions you are sure to be asked, is the dreaded, "When are you going to get married?" I am constantly bombarded with questions about my relationship status from full grown adults, asking, "Why are you still single Valerie? Valerie, what's going on? Is there anyone yet?"

Then there are the personal improvement tips: Dress a little differently. You're too intimidating, so stop that. Your heels are too high, so you look too tall. Be more open and on and on....

I mean, if you listen to these well intentioned people long enough, you will seriously start to think that maybe there is something wrong with you.

What they can't seem to understand is that regardless of my relationship status, just as I am, I am whole.

For a long time, I was waiting for my husband because I thought that my life would start once I got married. I was waiting for someone to rescue me and say, "Ok, Valerie, now live."

Thankfully, I didn't meet anyone for two years, which was a blessing because had I gotten a husband or even into another relationship, like I wanted to, I wouldn't be where I at the place where I am today...free ... free to choose and to decide for myself who I want to be and what I want to create in my life.

> *I am ... free...free to choose and to decide for myself who I want to be and what I want to create in my life.*

Thank God

After the broken engagement and the initial relief of getting out of something that would have been really bad, I realized that I was heartbroken. And not just heartbroken, I was shattered. I couldn't understand it because I was praying for all those years asking God if Manny was the one and yet it took so long for me to get it and see that he was not the one. How come no one told me? How come I didn't hear?

Put a Smile On

The challenge in public relationships is that the breakups are public as well. Going to church, Sunday after Sunday, was hard because it felt like every time I walked in, there were people looking at me and watching to see how I was handling things. Was I going to crack or breakdown or spontaneously combust? They would watch, but would never ask me anything about the breakup, which was frustrating.

So, I did the only thing I knew to do. I always wore my best outfits, and made sure everything was in place, including my smile and an upbeat attitude, regardless of what I was really feeling inside. At the time, I was the director of the children's ministry, so I really had to keep it together. Most of the time, I just felt like screaming! When I really couldn't take it, I would run to the bathroom and cry, and when I was done, I would wipe my face and make sure that my smile was in place.

It Gets Better
"I wish I could fast forward my life and see if I actually made it through." Sexting in Suburbia, Lifetime Movie

Those were among the last words of a girl who committed suicide after being bullied by her schoolmates because of a mistake she made that they wouldn't let her forget.

Can I tell you a secret, that's not really a secret?

As long as you have breath in you, you have life. Right now at this very moment, you are alive, and as long as you have life in you, it is possible for things to turn around. Things are going to get better. This is the not the end of your story, the best is yet to come.

Because you have breath, you have an opportunity to watch things turn around. That's what makes suicide such a tragedy. How dare we give up on life! We still have life in us and what we are going through is temporary.

But I get it, because I remember I was at a point where I wanted to give up on my life because it was just not "fun" living anymore. And I would just pray: "Lord, just let me sleep for a really long time." See, I kinda wanted to die, but not really, because I would finish the prayer by saying, "but then I want to wake up again."

I would tell my friend all that time that I just didn't want to wake up, and she wouldn't even say anything because she didn't know what to say. I had a desire for life, but I didn't want to deal with my current circumstances. I didn't want to deal with the hurt and the disappointment. But I thank God for unanswered prayers because I would have missed life.

> When no one else was there, when it seemed like no one else cared and no one understood, I could ALWAYS turn to God ...and then there would be this peace...

You want to know why I love Jesus so much, and hold on so tenaciously to my faith? One of the reasons is because when no one else was there, when it seemed like no one else cared and no one understood, I could *ALWAYS* turn to God and cry and talk and write; and then there would be this peace, this knowing inside of me that everything was going to be alright. Little things would happen that would just let me know that He heard me. When I needed Him most, He was not this Awesome God that sat on His throne looking down at me and indulging me. He was my friend that stuck closer than a brother. There were certain places where I was, that I couldn't explain to people what I was feeling, because I didn't even know myself; , but my Friend knew and understood.

There are a lot of people who have gone through tough times and attempted suicide but they survived and today they are living to testify that it gets better. They can say with an assurance that suicide would have been a permanent deadly solution to a temporary problem.

I Found Joy

There are times when you can't see any light at the end of the tunnel. Perhaps you've had a bad day, a bad month, year or years so far; but, since you have life in you, you can rest assured that the story is not over yet, and that it is possible for things to turn around.

There used to be days when I would just start crying for no reason. I once saw some pigeons eating bread and I busted out in tears. My heart was broken. But then one day I stopped crying and realized that I had gotten through the day without tears! As a matter of fact, I didn't cry yesterday either. You see, while I wasn't looking, my heart was healing. While I wasn't looking, I found joy, which supersedes happiness, which is temporary and dependent on the external. Joy goes to the inner core of who you are and remains unaffected by life's circumstances.

One page can change how the story ends. The final chapter is unwritten. Don't quit before you see how the story ends.

I Needed a Change
I needed a change. And like an answer to an unspoken prayer, I found out about an opportunity to study abroad in Paris for a year. I didn't know how, I didn't know how much, and I didn't care. I was going.

Two months later, I was pulling my suitcase through JFK with my freshly acquired passport in my hand. I was so scared that I threw up in my uncle's car on the way to the airport. I took a year off from school, stepped down as the director of the children's ministry, packed everything up, said goodbye to everyone and everything, and chose me.

> *One page can change how the story ends.*

With tears in both of our eyes, I kissed my mom goodbye and never looked back. As I walked down the corridors of JFK Airport, all I kept thinking was *Valerie, what are you doing? Are you crazy? You don't know anyone. You don't speak the language. And you're scared of planes. Remember. If you go back now, everyone would understand and your mom would be happy.*

As these thoughts were going through my mind, I almost turned around, but then I remembered what I would be going back to and that life behind me was no longer an option. So instead, I took one blurry step forward, and then another, and then another, and unbeknownst to me at the time, I was literally walking through to the other side of fear.

That was the day I got on the plane and landed in Paris, 8 hours later.

Turning Points

That moment was a major turning point in my life. There are moments throughout each of our lives that turn out to be turning points, moments cause a domino effect of change in our lives. They are the fork-in-the-road moments where decisions are made that can alter the course of our lives. Up until that point my turning points were:

> *turning points, moments that cause a domino effect of change in our lives.*

- becoming a Christian, which changed my identity
- Ending my engagement which freed me from people's opinions because I stood up for myself and made a decision for myself without permission from anyone.
- Studying abroad in Paris, which is where I defined for myself: who I was, and who I wanted to be; and where I decided that I was going to live on the other side of fear no longer striving for the approval of people

Kansas Is

Paris was one of the best decisions that I ever made, not simply because it was Paris, (though it was Paris :)), but because it was such a significant turning point. The first half of that trip was horrible. Paris in the winter was super depressing, or maybe it was just me. Either way, by December, I called my mom and told her that I was coming home. She was ecstatic and just needed to know when and where to come pick me up. I was working as an English tutor, so I called my boss to thank him for the opportunity and to tell him that I was leaving.

This man didn't exactly have the reputation of being a warm guy, but in that moment in time, he was a godsend. He told me a story about when he was hitchhiking across the country and when he was done, he asked me one question - "When you leave and go back home and people ask you how was Paris, what are you going to say?"

Up until that point, I spent a majority of the time in bed watching American movies. I hadn't even *experienced* Paris.

After deciding to stay, I got a new host family, who were amazing, and moved into my own place for the very first time. I was exposed to such an array of French cuisine including frogs legs, very thin slices of raw meat with the blood pooled in a corner of the plate, slightly boiled eggs that you crack at the top and dip strips of bread in and eat etc... I even made lifetime friends who I am still close with today.

By the time I got back home, whenever people asked me "how was Paris?" I had so much to say, all because I decided to stay and made up my mind to be open.

Welcome Back

Within a year of coming back home, I got my Bachelors in Social Work, got accepted to graduate school, studied abroad in Spain for a month, came home, and the following week flew out to Arizona for my first ever self-development conference. The next week, I went to Disney World with 7 members of my family, after getting an all-expense paid 5-day trip. After Disney World, I started graduate school, began a photography business, flew out to California that November for my second conference, came back home and continued graduate school, flew out to California in March for my third conference, came back, graduated with my Masters in Social Work and decided that instead of getting a 9-5 job I was going to pursue my passion and start my own business equipping young women to live a life of standards, success and service. Whew!

It wasn't all smiles and good times, but I really was content and had joy.

I Am Free from Other's Expectations

Often times you can care too much about what others think about you and you allow their opinions and expectations to hold you back and keep you from make the best decision for you. Life is long, but it is too short to constantly live under the constraint of other's expectation.

You have to let that go.

One day while sitting at the kitchen table, I had an epiphany: I don't have to be married to move out. Growing up there were many expectations for women. One of the expectations was that you don't leave your parent's house till you are married, no matter how old you are. I have spoken to so many women who tell me about how they got married in order to escape their home life.

> *Life is long, but it is too short to constantly live under the constraint of other's expectation.*

I use to be so frustrated about being single because I thought I would end up at my mom's house forever. The night I had my epiphany I shared it with my mother and she just looked at me as if I had lost my mind. She didn't like it, but that's the beauty of being free from other's expectations.

So many times you put your life on hold waiting to get married and end up settling because you're tired of being single, but that's not the answer! There are so many women married and frustrated because the made a desperate choice.

Do I want to get married? Sure do. I look forward to it and I look forward to the privileges that come with marriage; but till that time comes, you better believe that I will continue living and enjoying life and all that it has to offer.

Your time to walk down the aisle and say I Do may someday come, but don't do it prematurely and don't do it out of desperation or for liberation. Some of you are already married, but it doesn't mean that it is too late to find the I Am Beautiful in you. Whatever your relationship status is, appreciate the beauty that this stage of your life is offering and know that it is possible to be whole and content.

I Am *Beautiful*

Beautiful is not how you look
Beautiful is not how you walk
Beautiful is not what you do
Beautiful is who you are
And you just being you
That is beautiful.
Valerie Jeannis, Just You 2012

☙❧

I AM Beautiful.

If only I believed that growing up, maybe I would have made different choices.
Maybe I wouldn't have settled for the things I did.
Maybe... but I didn't. So as a result, I held on to any guy that made me feel as though I was beautiful.

Mickey Mouse & the Tall Green Giant

I will never forget the day I walked into class and everyone started laughing. It was Picture Day in the 6th grade and that morning I told my mom that I would be styling my hair myself, and for some reason, she agreed. The last thing I ever expected was that everyone would start laughing. After standing frozen for a moment, I hurried to my seat and just died inside.

All of this was because I had a crush on Rascal, one of my classmates, who absolutely did not feel the same way about me. To make sure everyone knew it, he started making fun of me. It didn't take long for them to come up with the perfect nicknames. Since my hairstyling knowledge was limited, every time I styled my hair, it ended up looking like Mickey Mouse ears, which is how I got the lovely nickname, Mickey Mouse. Then there was the forest green coat that my bought me (you know, the types that last forever and ever!) since I was one of the tallest girls in my class at the time, I also got the name, Tall Green Giant.

As if that wasn't bad enough, one day while I was walking with my aunt, she turned to me and said - "You would have been pretty if you had hair."

What do you say to that?

I just smiled and kept on walking.

My Chris Tucker

Once that school year ended, I told my mother never again. Never again would I have a year like that one. I decided that I was going to get braids. But before I did, I met my Chris Tucker. Rush Hour just came out and I could have sworn I was in love with Chris Tucker because he was so funny. One day while visiting my cousin, I met this guy who to me looked like Chris, big eyes and all.

That summer we all went to camp together, and he actually liked me back... ME with my Mickey Mouse hair.

He liked me when everyone else thought I was ugly. Oh he wasn't going anywhere. As far I was concerned, it was love and he became my first boyfriend.

Things were a changing.

The first day of 7th grade, I walked into the school, fresh braids and all, and the guys including Rascal, were standing in a corner. When they looked up, I overheard them say, "Who's that girl?" IT WAS ME!!!!

Oh I was on top of the world!

I liked the attention – at first - but then I started feeling really bad about myself because the guys were just interested in what they wanted and hoped to get from me, but none of them were really interested in *me*.

My Chris would say all these nice things when it was just the two of us, but when he got around others it was a totally different story. He would talk bad about me and make fun of me in front of his friends as though he was ashamed to like me. And yet I still stayed. It was an on again off again, flirtation that went on for years. For a long time, I just didn't know how to say goodbye because he liked me first.

Man! At the time, I would have given anything for things to work out between us, but it didn't and looking back I am so grateful to God for that unanswered prayer.

Someone who cares about you would not talk bad about you when other people are around and would not make you feel bad about yourself.

If I had believed that I was beautiful, I would not have been swayed by the first guy (or any guy) who said it.

Beloved, you cannot wait for someone to tell you, you have to learn to tell yourself, regardless of how you are feeling!

> *At some point you have to be able to look at yourself and not only say that you "I Am Beautiful, but know that "I Am Beautiful."*

The Weight Thing

At some point you have to be able to look at yourself and not only *say* that "I Am Beautiful", but *know* that "I Am Beautiful".

It's not always easy to believe when you not only have to deal with outside people's opinion but also the opinions of your family and those who say they love you. When you come home to the criticisms and there is no escape, its torture; and it just hurts.

I never had a weight issue till after the big breakup. I went from a size 4/6 to a 10/12 in such a short amount of time and gained over 40lbs.

Most of the weight gain took place while I was away, so when I came back home after a year, let's just say it was noticed. I didn't start feeling bad about it till it seemed like everyone was making comments. Every time I went to go get a plate of food or touched the fridge, it would be a look, a sound or a comment.

And listen, I get that some people were concerned because they cared about me, but when things are said the wrong way, it makes it hard to hear.

It was a struggle because, while I was battling people, I had my personal battles. None of my clothes fit. So every time I got dressed it was like a demoralizing ceremony. I would start to put one thing on, it would get half way; so I would have to pull it off, throw it in a pile and reach for the next thing. And with each article of clothing that I had to pull off, I just felt worse and worse. The crazy thing is that I refused to buy new clothes because I didn't want to accept the weight.

It got to the point where I even tried throwing up once, but I snapped out of it because I didn't want to compromise my mental and physical health and put myself on a destructive path that would be so hard to recover from. Nothing good comes from deliberately going down that path. But the fact that I attempted it was a wakeup call for me, so I made a decision and signed up for boot camp. Every morning for a month, I woke up at 4:30am to get to boot camp. It was worth it, because I lost 20+, but it didn't seem to matter because the comments didn't stop.

If those who loved us really knew and understood the impact of their words and how they hurt instead of motivate, they would stop and find another way.

It is so sad to know that so many feel pushed into a corner where they feel like the only alternative is to make themselves sick in order to fit some image and have someone else decide that they are okay.

> *I Am Beautiful is necessary because when you don't believe it for yourself, you will be thrown back and forth like the waves in a wind storm of people's opinion.*

It took a long time for me to be able to look at myself in the mirror and say, "You know what Valerie, just the way you are, you are beautiful and I love you."

I Am Beautiful is not about being conceited or self-centered but it's about self-love. It's about knowing that you are more than enough and that you do not need validation from someone else, because you validate and esteem yourself.

I Am Beautiful is necessary because when you don't believe it for yourself you will be thrown back and forth like the waves in a wind storm of people's opinion. It is a dangerous and lonely thing when you are living for someone else's approval!

I AM BEAUTIFUL

Every day we are bombarded with images of what someone else defines as beauty. Regardless of what you look like, according to the media's standards, you never feel good enough. And if you do, you are so scared of losing it, that you put yourself through all this stuff, just to hold on to that coveted spot. It is way too hard living up to someone else's definition of what is beautiful.

Song of Myself

My poem, Song of Myself, was inspired by the people I saw along the walk of life and *the me* I saw in them.

> *I saw...*
> *The girl enviously looking at the person across from her, dejecting herself and wishfully praying for a beauty so perfect, with the misconstrued notion that it'll be the answer to all her prayers*
> *The goddess whose immaculate grandeur, which is so often seen as a blessing, is her most prominent curse*
>
> *I saw...*
> *The troubled teen whose cries for help fall on deaf ears*
> *The girl who gets frightened by her reflection, because for a brief moment she forgets that under all the make-up, without the contacts, fake hair, fake eyelashes, fake beauty mark, the piercings, tattoos, and the "in" clothes, it's just her*
> *The one lying in the hospital because, since she didn't look like that beautiful actress, life just wasn't worth living.*

This is real! We need to fall in love with ourselves. We need to recognize that truly "I Am Beautiful" because if you don't, the price that *you* may end up paying just to hear someone else call you beautiful, may be more than you ever thought and way more than you could have ever imagined you would have to pay..

Listen, I love to have fun and I love to dress up. One of the great things about being a girl is that we have so many options. I can wear makeup, change up my hair, try fun clothes on and cool shoes. It is one of the great benefits of being a girl; and I do it all. But it's so important to me that when I take off all the makeup, the fake hair, the fake eyelashes, the jewelry, and the clothes that I can still look at all of me and say "Yes, I Am Beautiful."

Just as you are, you are beautiful. Whatever size you wear, you are beautiful. No matter what people say, you are beautiful. And because you love yourself, you will treat yourself right, which includes being in optimal health, staying fit, dressing yourself right, feeding yourself right. And as you love you, you will settle for no less from any other person.

As you fall in love with you, you will realize and recognize that you are worth it, and that you deserve, and are worthy of, great things.

I Am *Loved*

If I knew that the last time was the last time
I would have hugged you tighter
Memorized your face with my hands
Kissed you more
If I knew that the last time was the last time
I would have held on longer
Measured my hands against yours
Told you how much I loved you
If I knew that the last time was the last time
I would have went back one more time
I would have kissed you goodbye
If I close my eyes
I can see you standing in the doorway of the hospital room
Watching me walk away
I wonder if you knew that it was the last time
I wonder what your final thoughts were
If I knew that the last time was the last time
I would have ran back
Hugged your legs
Told you I loved you
And kissed you goodbye
Valerie Jeannis, Goodbye 2005

Dads Are Just Good For Money

It was a Saturday morning, and I was on the phone with my best friend when I told her, "Dads are only good for money." At the time, that's all mine seemed to be good for anyway.

Valerie Jeannis

I loved my dad but he was rarely there. He left my mom when I was three months old and got a whole new family, which never left him with enough time for me. He use to pick me up in the mornings and take me to school, but there were so many days where I would sit on the window ledge waiting for his taxi to pull up to the building, but nothing. My mom would eventually have to come and tell me that we had to go because he wasn't coming.

In spite of everything, every time it was my birthday, he would always be there and bring me a Hallmark card with $100 in it; and bring my brother and sister with him, so we could get to know each other.

One of my favorite things was when my dad would drop by and see me. I was always excited when he showed up. Before he even got to the door, I would run out and meet him, and he would pick me up and carry me inside. After he put me down, I would run to the bathroom and grab the big red comb, sit in back of him on the sofa, take his hat off and comb his hair.

I guess he figured that there would always be time later for us to connect, but he was wrong.

I don't remember how I found out my dad was sick; but I do remember visiting him in the hospital with my mom and godmother. He looked fine to me. When we were leaving, his large frame filled the door post as he watched us go.

I waved goodbye and went to the lobby to wait for my mom. My godmother came up to me and asked me to go back with her so she could say goodbye. Since I already said bye, I said, "No," and chose to stay in the lobby instead.

That will forever be one of my biggest regrets, because that was the last time I saw my dad alive.

But He Was Fine

I use to be a first base catcher on a softball team, and one Friday during a practice game, my mom came to pick me up early. As I walked off the field, I looked at my mom and just knew. When I asked her, "did he die?" she was surprised by the question, but she said, "Yes." Right there in the middle of the street, I broke down in tears because I lost the father I never knew. He was only 42 years old, and he was fine the last time I saw him!

After he died, it was weird because it seemed like nothing had changed. He wasn't there before, and he wasn't there now. One day after school, I saw his taxi driving by, and I ran after it, till the car finally stopped and I saw the driver's face. That was not my dad, and it would never again be my dad. That's when it really hit me that I would never see him again.

There were so many questions. Why did you walk away from me and my mom? Why weren't you around more? Why did you have to die?

The one thing that bothered me the most was that I don't remember ever saying, "I love you" to him, or hearing him say, "I love you" to me.

He must have though, because everyone said he did.

Hot Potato, Stop

When my mom found out she was pregnant with me, she hadn't been in the US long and didn't speak English. In order to provide for me, she had to go to school, work at an overnight job, and figure out what to do with me. I ended up living with my baby sister and then a family friend; and then on the weekends, I eventually was able to stay with my mom.

In spite of how I felt, I was loved.

There would be days when I would wake up and think that I was back home with my mom, but then I would remember where I was and have to deal with the feelings of frustration and disappointment.

I hated not living with my mom and was angry about it. It just wasn't the same living with other people. I never really spoke up for myself much, but I was quietly defiant. If something was unfair, I would do little things to vent.

I thought it was unfair that I always had to wash the dishes, and since I couldn't say no, I would wash them, but I always made sure that I "accidently" broke one dish. (I think the first time it really was an accident.) In any case, I eventually no longer had to wash dishes.

I was also really aggressive; so I was usually in trouble. My punishment would mainly involve me being confined to a room by myself.

For a long time I felt like a hot potato that no one wanted, which made it hard to feel loved. I had to learn that in spite of how I felt, I was loved. It would be so easy to focus on the bad stuff and the hurts; but it wasn't all bad. There were nights when I would stay up with the older kids, and we would sneak into each other's room and spend the whole night talking till we saw the sun rise; and then we would go to bed.

Everyone wants love, to love and to be loved, whether they know it or not, whether they recognize it or not.

We would also put on performances and shows; and when it was someone's birthday they would be the king or queen for the day, and their wish would be our command. Those were great moments.

He First Loved Me
"We love Him, because He first loved us." 1 John 4:19

Have you ever been looking for something: I mean really searching high and low and turning everything over just to find that thing; then just when you are about to give up and sit down, you look up and the thing that you were looking for was right there all long? It is absolutely frustrating!

Everybody wants love, to love and to be loved, whether they know it or not, whether they recognize it or not. When you think about it, a lot of the things that we do and mistakes that we make, usually (but not always) stem from a desire to be loved and accepted.

When I first became a Christian, I wanted to be *so good* because I wanted God to love me and I didn't want Him to stop. So, I thought that by doing all these things, I could make God love me; but then I really started reading and believing this verse:

"We love Him, because He first loved us." 1 John 4:19

Then there's another verse which says, *"...while we were yet sinners, Christ died for us."* Romans 5:8

And just in case I still didn't get it, I found another verse which said,

> [35] *Who shall separate us from the love of Christ? Shall tribulation, or distress, or persecution, or famine, or nakedness, or peril, or sword?* [37] *Nay, in all these things we are more than conquerors through him that loved us.* [38] *For I am persuaded, that neither death, nor life, nor angels, nor principalities, nor powers, nor things present, nor things to come,* [39] *Nor height, nor depth, nor any other creature, shall be able to separate us from the love of God, which is in Christ Jesus our Lord.* Romans 8:35, 37-39

I AM BEAUTIFUL

Right there in God's Word, I found the thing that I was searching for the whole time: a love that was unconditional, and that was not dependent on me being anything other than who I was, and even when I messed up, it was ok because He STILL LOVED ME.

I love the story of David one of Israel's kings. Here was a man who was disobedient, who lied, committed adultery, murder, and fornication; and even after all that, God said, "Here is a man after My own heart!" God loved him because God's love was unconditional, and in spite of what David did, God's view of David was never going to change. Now *that's* a love that I can count on and find safety in!

Waiting for Me

I learned to love me.

Somewhere along the way, I lost my love for me. I don't know how or how long it took or even what triggered it, but I do remember one day saying, "You know what, I like me. I started thinking about all the things that I liked about myself, and by the end of the list I had to declare, I love me. Sometimes it doesn't have to be more complicated for that. I learned to love me.

I Am Loveable

This one is still the hardest to believe because things just didn't always work out, but yet still, I am lovable and I am loveable simply because *I Am*.

PS. So are you!

Valerie Jeannis

I Am *Forgiven*

"As far as the east is from the west, so far has he removed our transgressions from us." Psalm 103:12

‍

Have you ever been caught red-handed doing something you know you weren't supposed to be doing? It is the worst feeling. You have no excuses and no defense. You're just plain guilty.

Scandalous

I have been there more times than I can count, because I wasn't always too good at following the rules. There was this one time during my crazy teen years that stood out above the rest. I was dating this beautiful, caramel skin, wavy hair, tall - just beautiful guy. One day while my mom was at work, he came over and we were sitting on the couch watching TV, talking and really *just* hanging out, when we heard keys outside the door. In hindsight, we should have just stayed sitting but I panicked. She walked in, took one look at me and went straight to my room, and there he was spilling out of the closet where I told him to go hide, since I wasn't supposed to have any guys in the house while she wasn't home. She just turned around, closed the door and walked out without saying a single word. Not yelling. Nothing.

After she left, I lost it. I broke down in tears and Mr. Caramel just stood there looking at me. This guy was not even worth it. Not only did I lose my mother's trust, but everyone assumed the worst. It was horrible.

That night I went to bed and was awakened by my uncle, (who lived 3 hours away!) storming into my room and just giving it to me.
I stayed under the covers and watched him as he yelled and yelled.

You're Still Worth It
Come now, and let us reason together, saith the LORD: though your sins be as scarlet, they shall be as white as snow; though they be red like crimson, they shall be as wool. Isaiah 1:18

If you saw a $100 bill on the floor and it was all covered in mud, been in the streets, stepped on and crushed and covered with dog's business, would you still want it?

Some of you are probably thinking "nope, I pass, thank you." But some of you are replying, "Give it to me, I know how to clean it right up."

What if in order to get it, you would have to reach into a puddle of NYC sewer water, which was bubbling in filth? Would you still want it?

In many ways I was like the $100 bill, covered with all that stuff and there were many people who thought I was too bad and not worth reaching for, but there was Someone who thought that I was still worth it. I am guilty of a lot of things, and my punishment would have been justified. Thank God for forgiveness!

There may be people who will try to throw things in your face and constantly try to remind you of the things you did; but someone's opinion of you does not have to be your reality. Your own mind may try to tell you that you are still the same person, but you are not. You are forgiven. Your slate has been wiped clean. None of us deserve it, but love did it for us anyway.

You might as well forgive yourself; because you serve no one by sitting in prison after the Judge declares that you are free. Do not allow yourself to be caged in by your own guilt.

Forgive Us Our Trespasses

"Forgive us our trespasses as we forgive those who trespass against us." Matthew 6:12

Forgiveness is usually easier said than done because there are some cuts that go deep; in spite of that, we are all challenged to forgive, especially if we want to be forgiven.

How do you forgive the person who is supposed to love you and have your back, when they are the one who betrayed you? How do you forgive when you come face-to-face with your tormentor?

There was a Holocaust survivor, who stood before an audience of thousands, sharing her story about the death of her family and her experience at concentration camps, when she suddenly just froze and went pale. Part of her presentation was about forgiveness and letting go when a man started approaching her with tears in his eyes. When he reached her, he said, "you don't know me, but I was a former SS Guard (one of the guards at the concentration camps), and I just want to apologize to you and ask you for forgiveness for all I've done." What he didn't realize was she *did* know him, because he was a guard at the camp she was at with her family.

> *Sometimes all you can do is reach out your hands and trust God to do the rest.*

What could she do when every part of her wanted to hate him, but the God in her said, "forgive him?" She did the only thing she could do; she reached out her hands robotically and put it in his outstretched hands. She shared that as she reached out her hands, God did what only He could do, which was soften her heart and allow her forgiveness to start to take place. At the end of it all, they were both in tears (along with most people in the audience) and they both got something that needed so desperately, the peace that comes from finally letting go and accepting forgiveness.

Sometimes all you can do is reach out your hands and trust God to do the rest.

It's easier said than done; but it is possible.

You may think that if you forgive, then that means that you will have to restore relationships or become friends; but not necessarily. Forgiveness is a must! But what takes place after that is a choice. There can be restoration or peaceful separation, which frees you from an intimate relationship with the person, and allows you to release all hostility.

Just let it go.

It is that hard, and that simple. Let it go.

Valerie Jeannis

I Am *Worth It*

Don't you know?
Have they not told you?
Didn't you see the memo?
You are Royalty.
Valerie Jeannis, Royalty 2012

ഓരു

Legend has it that in the 1950s a group of Tibetan monks were informed that a highway was being built, and the highway would have to go through the location where the shrine for which they were responsible was currently located. The shrine, a huge clay Buddha, would have to be moved. Arrangements were made and the day of shrine moving arrived. The shrine, located under a roof to keep it safe from the elements, was prepared for its journey. A crane began lifting the clay Buddha. The Buddha, as it rose off of its block resting place, began to crack. It was much heavier than all the engineers had estimated. They needed a larger crane, which meant they had to wait until the next day. The Buddha would have to spend the night in its current location. To make matters worse, there was a storm brewing and the next day would be a stormy one.

The monks covered the Buddha with waterproof tarps on poles to keep it dry overnight. During the night, the head monk awoke and decided to check on the Buddha. With a flashlight, the monk carefully checked the condition of the Buddha. As he walked around the huge clay figure shining his light on the cracks, something caught his eye. He returned to the spot on which he had just shined his light. He peered into the crack and could not believe his eyes. After hours of chiseling, the monks stepped back and stared in awe at the sight before them. There, in front of the monks, stood a solid gold Buddha.

This statue which everyone originally thought was clay, turned out to be gold. Kind of like you and I. We look at ourselves sometimes and see an average person, but what don't see is that beneath the surface there is gold. There is more to you than what quickly meets the eye.

That statue is valued today at over $200 million dollars.

Can you imagine going through life as a lump of clay when you are actually solid gold!!

The fact is, that's how most of us go through life; but now it's time to take a second look. Don't be surprised when you discover that you are so much more, and worth so much more than you ever thought; and now that you know better, you can make some new choices.

Get Off the Tree

During one of my walks through Central Park, I saw a young girl leaning against a tree making out with some guy who was pushed up on top of her. They couldn't have been older than 6th graders. A few feet away, a group of their friends were cheering them on.

I AM BEAUTIFUL

Have you ever seen those moms who show up at their kids' school with their house coat on and rollers in their hair, in a rage, ready to snatch their kids up? Well, I was having one of those moments, as I look observed what was going on. All I wanted to do was walk up to the girl and say "don't you know that you are worth it? Don't you know who you are? That you deserve the best? This is not your place beloved; you are worth so much more." I wanted to, but I didn't. As I was looking at her, it was as though I was looking at me. I was never on a tree but there was a train.

If only we knew better. Not simply head knowledge, but really knew better. If only we believed that we were worth it, then there would be no room for settling.

It's easier said than done, of course; but once you start changing the way you see you, that will lead you to changing the way you see your world, and everything else around you. That will make all the difference. That's what made the difference for me.

Reset

Every single time the transportation fare is raised, everything is reset to take the new fare. Whether you're using change on the bus, or a metro card in the train station, the minute that the new fare is put into effect, everything is already switched over.

It doesn't matter what you use to do in the past, or who you use to do it with; you get to decide what is now acceptable. $1.25 is not going to get you anywhere in NYC now-a-days because the price has gone up. There was a change. If you decide that you want to change, you get to set a new standard.

That's Not Fair

Growing up there were certain things that bothered me and one of them was the way boys were treated and put on a pedestal by the woman in our family.

I don't know if it's a Caribbean thing or if it is something that transcends culture but as a female, it was infuriating. Whenever we sat down to eat, our grandmother would prepare the nicest table setting for our boy cousin. He would get the best and biggest pieces of meat, and however he wanted his meal prepared is how he got it. And I don't know about my other cousins, but I would sit there looking at this fiasco thinking, "Shoot, I'd like my food prepared that way too."

One day, I actually asked her about it and let's just say it was the last time I voiced my observation.

I AM BEAUTIFUL

As I got older, I noticed that I carried that the injustice of the family's inequity in many parts of my life. I was always a saver, but when it came to gifting someone I was in a relationship with, I would always give them the best

One day I bought two pairs of shoes for my boyfriend (just because) and when I gave them to him, not only did he not appreciate them; all I got in response was an, "oh," which really made me mad since instead of getting anything for myself, I just thought of him. Plus, I never spent that much money on any shoes that I had bought for myself. That was my reality check! Turned out the shoes didn't fit him, which worked out perfectly because I went back to the store, returned both pairs of shoes, and bought 1 pair of shoes that were worth more than the two pairs for him put together...for ME!

We need to learn how to treat ourselves better. It is not selfish, but self-fulfillment! If you are willing to do it for somebody else, then you need to be willing to do it for yourself. You are worth it. You can't spend your life waiting for someone to do it for you and then get mad when they don't. Besides, you're ability to love yourself will set the standard for how others will love you and will enable you to extend healthy love to others.

One of the Golden Rules is to "*love your neighbors as yourself*" Matthew 12:21, KJV. If you can't love you, how can you extend healthy love to others?

You Are Worth It

I remember the day that my mom gave herself permission to be worth it. She needed some new glasses; and after she tried all the reasonably priced ones (aka. The ugly cheap ones), there was a nice pair of Fendi glasses that caught her eye. Even though she knew she liked them, she felt guilty for spending all that money on a pair of glasses for herself. She almost chose something else; but after a quick pep-talk, she chose herself and got the glasses. And let me tell you, when she has her glasses on, she feels like a million bucks! She literally walks differently because she feels that good about the way she looks.

We need to learn how to treat ourselves better. It is not selfish, but self-fulfillment!

Why aren't we giving ourselves permission to experience that all the time? It doesn't require spending a lot of money or doing something extravagant. Sometimes it's the little things…!

No matter what it is that you decide to do, always remember that you are worth it; so stop settling for the practical.

I Am *Grateful*

Thank you.

෫෬

In the midst of all our goals and focus, all the things we have to do and the promises we made – the assignments that must be submitted and bills that must be paid, in the midst of life – sometimes we forget to simply say thank you.

It's amazing how something as simple as gratitude can change your perspectives.

Thank You In Advance

My mom and I use to live in a 1 bedroom apartment downtown New York; till she recognized that it was time for me to have my own room. So we moved into the "projects" when I was in the junior high. It was a nice apartment but unfortunately the tenants in the building did not keep the common areas clean. For years we would get really irritated every time we saw the mess, but then I started changing my perspective. Instead of getting frustrated every time I would get on the elevator and see pee on the floor, I decided to say thank you in advance. I started thanking God for the testimony and would start declaring that when I move into my personally owned home, this is going to be such a great story. That little change made all the difference.

No matter what you're going through or what has taken place, there's always a reason to say "thank you."

Finding Purpose in Pain
"All things work together for good" Romans 8:28, KJV

Often times the hardest moments of our lives reveal our life's call and purpose. I am grateful for every broken road because they can usher you to where you were meant to be, IF YOU LET IT.

One day while I was at work, I got a call from my boyfriend, and after getting into the same ol' argument; I broke down and started crying. I pulled out a legal pad and pen, and I just started writing. I was so mad because I couldn't help but think if I had a wise older woman giving me advice, I wouldn't be in this relationship.

That was the day that I started developing a program for young women to help them live a life of standards and to just be whole people. That was the day, the League of Extraordinary Young Women was conceived, though I didn't know the name at the time. I wanted young girls to know that they are so beautiful and special and destined for so much more. I wanted them to know that they never had to settle for anything less, and that they were worth waiting for. I wanted them to know the power that they possessed, even though at that time, I wasn't able to tap into mine and get out of that relationship.

That was the day I learned that there is purpose in pain.

Thank You for My Mom

After I graduated with my MSW, I decided not to get a job because I made up my mind to pursue my dream of starting a program aimed at helping young women achieve success earlier in life. Everyone thought I was crazy because they couldn't understand why I made the choice that I did.

My mom didn't understand my choice, but she backed me up anyway. One of the greatest gifts that she gave me was the space and permission to pursue my dreams. Had it not been for her support, I would have still made it, but it would have most likely been later on in life.

Gratitude Walks

One of my favorite things to do is go on *gratitude walks*. You just walk around saying, "thank you" for everything that you see, and whatever else comes to mind.

Thank you for love and forgiveness
For spring time and new hope
For friends and family
New friends and opportunities
I am grateful for the ability to smile
And walk and talk and hear and see and smell and touch and feel
Thank you for water and heat and an air conditioner and a home
For tiled floors to walk on and indoor plumbing
For the ability to write and comprehend and understand new things

Valerie Jeannis

Thank you for pens and paper and books and libraries
Thank you for faith and communities of support
Thank you for life and breath and the ability to choose

Thank you. Thank you. Thank you.

I Am *Alive*

I heard the charge and I seized it
I claim my joy back
I claim my enthusiasm back
I claim my life back
I Am Alive
Valerie Jeannis, 2012

One morning while I'm in the bathroom brushing my teeth, my mom walked in half asleep. She sat down with her eyes closed and began rubbing the crown of her back. I turned to look at her and was overcome by a sudden wave of sadness. As I studied her face, it was as if she was praying, "Lord, please just get me through this day."

I couldn't help but wonder how many of us are just "getting through the day" and how many more will wake up and find that they have gotten through their life without ever really living or enjoying their life. There was a research study which stated that most people die by the age of 21 and aren't buried till they are in their 60s.

Reality Check

We're only given one life to live and after that is death. The reality is you're going to die. All of us are.

Harsh? Perhaps, yet true nonetheless. But there's good news. Right now, you get to choose what kind of life you are going to live, who you want to be. What are you going to do with this one life you've been given?

After finding out she was dying of cancer, in one of her final performances, Poet Gabrielle Bouliane said…..

> —What are you waiting for? Why aren't you being everything that you can be right now? Why haven't you asked that crush you have out on a date? Or applied for your motorcycle license? Or told your family you're going back to school to become the one career you've always wanted to become, whether it's sensible or not?
>
> I know you've heard it a thousand times: You only get one life. Let me rephrase that in a way that will make more sense: You're going to die, sometime, somehow. The only difference between you and me is that I may have an idea of when and how . . . Do not wait . . . Start today and change your life to the best it can be.

So what are you going to do with this one life you've been given?

It's time for you to make up your mind that you are not going to simply get through life or let life pass you by.

You Survived Now Thrive

Many of you have made it through unbelievable challenges and are without a doubt survivors, but now it's time to thrive. It's time to dream again. It takes as much energy to dream a big dream as it does to dream a small dream. So dream big. Get excited about life and being alive. Get curious. Try something new.

We All Have Our Own Path

Each and everyone one of US was created for a purpose, which is as unique as each of our fingerprints. You cannot copycat someone else's purpose; and why would you want to? All of our journeys are different, which is what makes life so beautiful.

> There's a script for each and every one of our lives, and it's up to us to identify what it is and then live it out.

I love the story of Dancing Matt. Here is a guy who was working at a job which he hated, and every day he would do some silly dance in front of his friend's desk, when it was lunch time to get his attention. One day his friend says, "Why don't you go do that dance somewhere else?" which is exactly what he eventually did. He cashed in his life's savings, took the money, his girlfriend and his camera and traveled around the world doing his silly little dance. That was in 2006. Six years later, he is still dancing all over the world, making people smile, and in his own unique way, bringing back hope to many.

There's a script for each and every one of our lives, and it's up to us to identify what it is and then live it out.

Valerie Jeannis

We've each been given something. Whenever you get an idea for something, whether a poem, book, play, movie or whatever, you have to know that it was given to you and only you. You need to have the mindset that if I don't do it, then nobody else will because no one else can. There is somebody who needs to hear or be exposed to whatever it is that you were given. So write the vision, make it plain and just go for it, because none of us were created to be on the sidelines of life.

I AM BEAUTIFUL

I Am *Moving Forward*

It may have taken me a little longer to get here,
But I am successful.
I may not have been able to finish with my class,
But I am successful.
I may not have a million dollars in the bank yet,
But I am successful.
Even if I am not #1, I am successful.
Even if the only thing I did was choose to get out of bed each day,
I am successful.
And I am moving forward.
Valerie Jeannis

ಸಿಂಜ

According to Wikipedia, ever since track runner Derek Redmond was a teen, he had been preparing and training to be a record breaking Olympic Gold Medalist and he was well on his way. During the 1992 Olympic Games, after winning his quarter-final, he was running in the semifinals when about 250 meters from the finish, his hamstring snapped and he fell to the ground in pain. When the stretcher bearers came to take off the field, he didn't go with them because he wanted to finish his race. So he just started limping along the track till he was joined by his father who charged past security and together they finished the lap and the race.

That injury ended his career as a professional runner, but he had a choice to make: What are you going to do now?

What Are You Going To Do Now?

Things don't always work out as you plan or expect. That's a reality. But what happens after that defeat is your decision. Giving up should never be an option. No matter how the plan changes or who is no longer a part of the journey, it does not matter. Either you stay down or you get up. Either you go back to the drawing board and figure it out, or decide it's not worth the pursuit.

Derek Redmond could have given up, but instead, he became a part of the Great Brittan national basketball team and reached division 1 in the Great Britain rugby team. He now serves as Director of Development for sprints and hurdles for UK Athletics and also works as a motivational speaker. He was able to accomplish all those things because he refused to give up and decided that his story would not end with or because of a snapped hamstring.

It's Only Half Time

Your inability to let go of the past and to stop looking back is one of the things that stops you from moving forward. Too many times you keep trying to go back to do things differently and miss the fact that the game went on. Things happened that you didn't plan on, but it's ok because it is not the end, it's only half time.

One of my favorite things about sports is watching a team that didn't start a game off well turn things around and win the game. Every new quarter presents the players on both sides and opportunity to reassess, reposition and win. And the ones who are able to forget about what happened just seconds ago, be present in the moment, keep their eyes on the prize, give all they have, win.

You Can Do This
"I can do all things through Christ who strengthens me." - Philippians 4:13

There was a man who was walking by a row of elephants when he suddenly stopped, confused by the fact that these huge creatures were being held by only a small rope tied to their front leg. No chains, no cages. It was obvious that the elephants could, at any time, break away from the ropes they were tied to but for some reason, they did not. My friend saw a trainer nearby and asked why these beautiful, magnificent animals just stood there and made no attempt to get away.

"Well," he said, "when they are very young and much smaller we use the same size rope to tie them and, at that age, it's enough to hold them. As they grow up, they are conditioned to believe they cannot break away. They believe the rope can still hold them, so they never try to break free." My friend was amazed. These animals could at any time break free from their bonds, but because they believed they couldn't, they were stuck right where they were.

It's time to change your mind about who you are and what you can do. If you are ever going to be all that you were created to be, then you have to free yourself from the false boundaries and limitations created by the past. So many times you go through life thinking you can't do something because that's what someone told you or you may have tried something in the past that didn't work and you told yourself that you couldn't do it. Do not disqualify yourself.

Failing Forward

Every time you take a step forward or are faced with a decision that will have an impact on the direction of your life, there are usually those initial "what-if's".

> *You fall, you get back up, you learn and then you do it better.*

So many people get stuck in the quick sand of what-ifs. The best advice I got after planning for months and months for a project I was working on, was, "You're going to fail and you have your whole life to do it. So, you might as well just go for it."

Very inspirational, right? I know. But it actually was. It loosed me from the fear of failure. And just like a baby learning to walk, I took one wobbly step forward after another. So I just started walking on wobbly legs, just like a baby learning to walk.

You fall, you get back up, you learn and then you do it better.

Sometimes all you have is just a little bit, just enough to take the first step. That's ok. Take it, because as you do, the next step will reveal itself to you and then the next.

Your Steps Are Ordered

When my godson was about two years old, I took him to the park with his stroller and he decided that he wanted to push the stroller even though he couldn't see over it. I allowed him to do so. As he was pushing, my job was simple: guide him safely as he moves forward. Since I saw all the potential dangers that and pitfalls and walls; every time he was getting too close to danger, I would just slightly steer the stroller to make sure he stayed on path.

As we are moving forward, there are potential dangers all around us that if we really knew everything, we would be paralyzed by fear. But I have come to understand that every single step that I take is ordered. Much like my godson's steps were ordered even though he didn't realize it.

While on this journey of self-discovery and pursuit of your dreams, you have to know that you want this. You have to get so tired of where you are and of your current circumstances. Your desire for more has to be so great that it overrides the fear of the unknown.

Though None Go With Me

There will be many times along this journey when you will want to give up; whether it is because of fear of failure or fear of success or whatever else. It doesn't really matter what the reason is. Whenever that time comes, it's always nice if there is someone there that you can reach out to and get your boost; but if you can't find anyone, then you need to boost yourself and encourage yourself.

Don't use that as an excuse to stop. Do not stop. Slow down if you have to, but don't stop. Never stop till you get there, and even then don't stop. Celebrate. Then dream a new dream.

Birds of a Feather

Who you choose to connect with matters. Those who are around you shape you. The negative choices someone else makes can impact you. Guilty by Association is still guilty. Ignorance by Association is still ignorance. Laziness by Association is still laziness. Bitterness by Association is still bitterness. Promiscuousness by Association is still promiscuousness. Bullying by Association is still bullying. Drugging by Association is still drugging. Being a Player by Association is still being a player.

Intelligence by Association doesn't exist. Transformation by Association is still your own transformation, because it comes from a decision that only you can make. Success by Association is an illusion because you are the only one who can make the decision to be successful. Talented by Association is ridiculous! You cannot catch talent like catching a cold. Entrepreneur by Association would be great if it were possible. Even if you inherit a business, its future success is achieved through diligence, planning and discipline. Power by Association would be better referred to as Inherited Dictatorship! Authority is God-breathed and productive. Power is force bred through intimidation.

Gratitude by Association is like being glad your friend got something to eat, while you're still hungry. Rejoice in the success of others, but develop gratitude from within. Happiness by Association is a temporary state of bliss dependent upon current circumstances; but we should be glad when good things happen to others. You get it. The same way, if you choose to surround yourself with positive, forward moving and thinking people - with Dreamers who are taking action and people who believe and understand their worth, you will pull each other up.

TD Jakes once said, "Stop hanging around with people who make you feel smart because of how dumb they are. If you are the smartest person in your group, then you need a new group that will challenge and stretch you."

I am not saying to turn your back on anyone who doesn't see things the way you do; but I am saying that you have to know where you want to go, and you cannot allow anyone to stop you from getting there.

PooPoo Platter

I was once asked if someone was offering me a beautiful multi-ethic array of Asian, Italian, Persian, French, American, Thai, & Chinese poo-poo from all over the world, would I want some. She was sticking this imaginary poo-poo platter in my face and even though there was nothing there, I jumped back and told her not to put that in my face. Well when people try to impose their criticism and doubts on you, it's the same thing. If you wouldn't take a nice mix of poo from around the world, then why accept their negativity? You don't have to accept anybody's poo-poo no matter how they decorate it. It's time to push away from the table and say no thank you and walk away.

You have to understand that people's belief about what you can or cannot do is based many times on what they believe about themselves and the choices that they made. Who cares if no one believes in you? What do *you* believe about you? Because how you answer that question will determine everything from what you accomplish to what you accept in your life. What do you want? How bad do you want it? And what are you going to do to get it? What are you going to do with this one life you've been given?

I Am *Somebody*

You are Somebody.
You are more than where you came from.
You are more than enough.
Valerie Jeannis

☙❧

Some of you may be reading this and thinking that they are good ideas - just not for you. One of the hardest things is changing your mind about yourself and daring to believe that it is possible for you.

> Every single one of us has a story and every single one of our stories has the power to impact change.

If you were never told that it was possible, let this be an opportunity for you to fulfill a dream that you never knew you had.

Every single one of us has a story and every single one of our stories has the power to impact change. Often times we feel as though we are alone in our struggles, doubts, fears and hopes, but if we just to ask, we would find that many, if not all of us, share similar hopes and fears. It doesn't matter if you're young or old, black or white, educated or uneducated, rich or poor, married or single, all of us at one point or another ask "Am I enough?"

You Are More than Enough

One person who constantly felt the burden of that question was Whitney Houston as revealed to us at her funeral by her friend and Bodyguard co-star, Kevin Costner in his eulogy.

> "...from the first time she took center stage here as a teenager, (she was) flushed with the excitement that she had exceeded everyone's expectations and awesome promise of what was to come. (Yet she) still needed to hear from her mother about how she was received. Was she good enough? Could I have done better? Did they really like me? Or are they just being polite because they were scared of you, Cissy? These are the private questions that Whitney would always have that would always follow her..."

As she was getting ready to do the screen test for The Bodyguard, Costner said,

> "That was the first time I saw the doubt. The doubt creep into her that she would not be handed the part. She would have to be great. The day the test came I went into her trailer after the hair and makeup people were done, Whitney was scared. Arguably, the biggest pop star in the world wasn't sure if she was good enough. She didn't think she looked right. There were a thousand things to her

that seemed wrong. I held her hand and told her that she looked beautiful. I told her that I would be with her every step of the way, that everyone there wanted her to succeed, but I could still feel the doubt...

She took it all in and asked me if she could have a few minutes by herself and would meet me on the set. I was sure she was praying. After about 20 minutes later she came out. We hadn't said four lines when we had to stop. The lights were turned off, and I walked Whitney off the set and back to her room. She wanted to know what was wrong, and I needed to know what she'd done during those 20 minutes. She said, "Nothing." in only the way she could, nothing. So I turned her around so that she could see herself in the mirror and she gasped. All of the makeup on Whitney's face was running. It was streaking down her face and she was devastated.

She didn't feel like the makeup we put on her was enough so she'd wiped it off and put on the makeup that she was used to wearing in her music videos. It was much thicker and the hot lights had melted it. She asked if anyone had seen -- if anyone had, I said I didn't think so.

It happened so quick, she seemed so small and sad at that moment, and I asked her why she did it. She said I just wanted to look my best. It's a tree we can all hang from. Unexplainable burden that comes with fame, call it doubt, call it fear. I've had mine, and I know the famous in the room have had theirs. I asked her to trust me and she said she would. A half hour later she went back in to do her screen test and the studio fell in love with her. The Whitney I knew, despite her success and worldwide fame still wondered am I good enough? Am I pretty enough? Will they like me? It was the burden that made her great, and the part that caused her to stumble in the end.

Whitney, if you could hear me now I would tell you, you weren't just good enough; you were great…You weren't just pretty; you were as beautiful as a woman could be. People didn't just like you, Whitney, they loved you.

…So off you go, Whitney, off you go. Escorted by an army of angels to your heavenly Father, and when you sing before him don't you worry, you'll be good enough."

You may not be preparing to audition for a movie alongside a renowned star, but you may find yourselves in the same place, where you are asking, Am I good enough? Am I pretty enough? Do they like me?

My heart for you is that you know that you know that you are more than enough and that you do not ever allow anyone or anything else to tell you differently.

I AM BEAUTIFUL

You Are Significant

After my graduate school graduation, one of my cousins came up to me and said "Valerie, I am so proud of you. The first one Man. Your bachelors last year and now your masters. You make it look easy. Now I know it is possible for us too." After I heard that I went online and looked up a PhD program. He gave me wind under my wings. I didn't really know that anyone was watching me or paying attention. I didn't realize that my presence made a difference.

No matter where you are right now, there is someone who is looking up to you and trying to figure out how they can make it there, too!

My business coach once told me that "To the 3rd grader, a 5th grader is god." In other words, no matter where you are right now, there is someone who is looking up to you and trying to figure out how they can make it there, too!

A Simple Prayer

Someone was praying once and asked "God, help me to find my place. Help me to make a difference even if it's IN one person's life."

In a world that at times can make you feel so insignificant, many share the same prayer "Lord, help me to matter."

The answer to that prayer is as simple and as difficult as this:
- Don't EVER give up
- Just be you.
- Trust that you are more than enough
- And to those who dare, Pursue your dreams and passion with no apologies, no regrets, and no looking back.

You are somebody. You matter. Your presence matters. Your life matters. You are significant. You are somebody.

> Thank you. I'm thanking you for being you. Because you make us believe. Believe in what's good and right. Believe in second chances. - Fantasia, the movie

I Am *Powerful*

You don't have to be a victim of your past or your life.
You don't have to live in the shadow of your past.
You don't have to live under the voices of condemnation.
You can choose who you want to be today.
You get to choose how you respond to your past.
You can choose what you want from your life.
You get to choose to not simply exist, but to actually LIVE.

You have the power in you to be a creator.
You get to say yes to your life.
You get to say yes to your dreams.
You get to say yes to every good and perfect gift.
You get to say yes to you.

You are Somebody.
Somebody Powerful.
Valerie Jeannis, Somebody Powerful 2012

Everything that you need to become who you want to be and to create the life that you want, is inside of you.

No Longer A Victim

"Why are you crying about something that you can change?" – Valerie Jeannis

It is easy to sit around and complain about something but if you're ever going to get to where you want to be, then you are going to have to get off your rump and do something. You get to decide: Are you going to be a creator of your life or a victim in and of your life?

If you want to stay a victim of your life its simple, all you have to do is continuously ask why me? However, if you're ready to move from being victim of your life to creator, meaning, you're ready to start taking control of your life in spite of your circumstances, then no matter what comes your way, you need to constantly decide.

The creator says what can I do now? The victim says why me?
The creator says what do I want? The victim says why me?
The creator says what do I have and how can I make it happen? The victim says why me?

You Are Strong

Every single thing that you have been through, every challenge, every hardship, every disappointment and every failure, everything you survive makes you stronger.

Every time you choose to speak up and let your voice be heard, you get stronger.
Every time you act out of integrity, even though no one is around, you get stronger.
Every time you choose to keep moving forward and to stand up even though no one is standing with you, you get stronger.
Every time you practice your skill or develop your talents, you get stronger.

Every time you choose to be your best without holding back because you don't want others to feel bad, you get stronger.
Every time you stand up for what you believe, you get stronger.
Every time you stand up for someone who needs you, you get stronger.
No matter what comes you're way, regardless of the challenge or obstacle, you don't have to be afraid because you are strong and you will make it through.

Tough Stuff

Once while hanging out with my 2 year old godson, I blinked and in slow motion I watched the stroller tip back and his head bounce off the floor. He just laid there for about 3 seconds and then started crying.

As I looked him over, there was no crack, no blood or anything. After a little TLC, he was fine. He got a piece of chicken and it was as if nothing ever happened. I just stood back and watched him in amazement, thinking, "Man! God really knew what he was doing when He created us. We are so resilient."

When you look back at some of the things you've made it through, my goodness! You technically shouldn't be here, But YOU ARE. You may have gotten banged up in the past, but you're still here and you are stronger then you will ever know. So the next time you fall, get back up because you are made out of tough stuff.

Valerie Jeannis

I AM BEAUTIFUL

I Am *Extraordinary*

*If you don't figure out the something,
You will just stay ordinary,
And it doesn't matter what the something is,
A work of art or a taco or a sock
Just create something for you
And it's you out in the world,
Outside of you
And you can look at it or hear it
Or read it or feel it
And you'll know a little bit about you
A little more than anyone else`
Your business is to create. Doesn't even matter what you do.*
From the movie PS I Love You

ℰℭ

As I listen to those words and write them down, I suddenly feel like its ok.
 It's ok if things I do are recognized; it's ok if they aren't
It's ok if feelings are reciprocated; it's ok if they aren't.
It's ok if I sing well; it's ok if I don't.
It's ok if my dance steps are right; it's ok if they aren't.
But either way I will continue to do.
I will continue to feel.
I will continue to sing.
I will continue to dance.
Because not doing, not feeling, not singing and not dancing are not ok.
Not doing any of it would just make me ordinary.
Simply doing it all makes me extraordinary.

So as I close this letter, this book to you, my hope is simply this, that you will make up your mind and decide right now to be exactly who God created you to be. Beautiful.

My hope is that through my journey, you gained insight and clarity on yours and that you will be able to take away at least one thing that will make things a little brighter and that will give you the strength to hold on a little longer.

I have never cried as much as I did on this journey. There were many days when I questioned myself and questioned God. I was always asking myself if I was crazy for thinking that I could do this.

Today, as I am lying in bed and writing these closing words, I stand as a testimony that what God promised is true.

"They that sow in tears shall reap in joy." Psalm 126:5, KJV

In other words, your tears are down payments to a joy, peace and contentment that are promised, if you just hold on.

Before I close, I have one final poem for now, just for you, so receive it from my heart to yours.

Stand up and wipe your tears
Open your eyes
Now See
See what's happening
Look at what's taking place
Every shame is being erased

I AM BEAUTIFUL

For every sorrow and disappointment
An exchange is being made
There is a trade taking place

I will take your pain and give you healing
I will take your hurts and give you joy
I will take your fear and give you power
I will take your weakness and give you strength
I will take your loneliness and give you love

For every rejection you faced, I offer you acceptance
For everything you lost, I offer restoration
For everything that was stolen, I will give you a new thing
For every curse that was spoken, I speak over your life a blessing
I will take every bad and give you every good and perfect gift
For everyone that turned their back and for all those that left, I offer you My hand

It's a new season
So let the past go
The old things are passed
And all things are made new

Your name has changed
Because you are no longer the same

Beloved
Beautiful
You are fearfully and wonderfully made
You are Beautiful

Valerie Jeannis

You are fearfully and wonderfully made
You are Able
You are fearfully and wonderfully made
You are Powerful
You are fearfully and wonderfully made
You are Free
You are fearfully and wonderfully made
You are Whole
You are fearfully and wonderfully made
You are Extraordinary
You are fearfully and wonderfully made

So Live

Live Fearlessly
Live on Purpose
Live without Apology

I love you.

(Beautiful)

A Special Message:

"Information changes situation." Sounds a bit cliché, I know, but it's true.

It's time to bring back the message to our young women and youth that It IS Possible and that's exactly what I do through my REAL Talk Presentations, groups and training programs.

My goal is to reach at least 1 Million young people with the message of possibility and to do that, I need your help.

You can help spread the message by booking me to come speak at your organization or letting any organization that you are affiliated with know about the REAL Talk Presentations.

Together we can pave the way to success for the next generation.

I look forward to hearing from you and serving you and your community.

Valerie

Info@ValerieJeannis.com
347.871.3246

Valerie Jeannis

REAL Talk (TM) Presentations

(Standards * Success * Service)

Empowering Keynotes and Workshop Series for Young Women & Youth

By Speaker & Author & Life Coach
Valerie Jeannis, MSW

Transforming through information because...It Is Possible!

I AM BEAUTIFUL

About the Speaker

Valerie Jeannis is the founder of the League of Extraordinary Young Women, Creator of the I Am Beautiful Movement, and author of I Am Beautiful. She is on a mission to bring back the message to young women and youth that It Is Possible. It is possible to dream and to make your dreams a reality.

Unashamed to use her life as a teaching mechanism, Valerie's REAL Talk and in your face messages inspires communities to believe and invest in themselves and to just go for it.

Valerie has come a long way from the girl who was told at 14 that she would have a baby by the time she was 16. Not only does she have her Masters in Social Work with a special concentration in youth and adolescence, but she is now a respected speaker and positive role model on the ability to start over and make successful choices.

Valerie Jeannis

About REAL Talk

Youth motivational speaker, Valerie Jeannis, MSW, has designed REAL Talk empowerment keynotes, workshops and bootcamps to inspire and guide young women and youth (from middle school - college) to discover who they are and the power they possess to create the life of their dreams.

The core message is a simple yet powerful one - It Is Possible.

Using a combination of easy-to-understand principles, powerful transformational exercises, compassion coaching, inspiration and motivation, Valerie passionately delivers this simple, yet life changing message through a variety of topics and modalities. She encourages those she encounters and works with to reach their full potential in their personal, entrepreneurial and spiritual lives.

The presentations are available in a variety of formats:

- Keynotes
- 1 Hr.- Half day Workshops
- 1-Day Workshops: 9 AM - 3 PM
- 3-Day Workshops (our Signature Bootcamp)

Workshops are a great tool for school classes, community groups, parents and educators.

To Book Valerie Jeannis or to learn more about REAL Talk presentations contact us at Info@ValerieJeannis.com or 347-871-3246.

I AM BEAUTIFUL

REAL Talk KEYNOTES AND WORKSHOPS

Topics include issues and challenges that youth are facing.

Most Popular Topics include:
1. I Am Beautiful
2. I Dare to Dream

1) I Am Beautiful
This topic is available as a keynote, workshop and weekend Bootcamp.

There is greatness inside of each of our young people and in order for them to live it out, they need to discover who they really are and the power they possess to create the life they want.

Valerie explores personal beliefs and the impact they have on various aspects of our lives. She also helps the audience start to discover who they are and the power they possess to create the life that they want.

2) I Dare to Dream
This topic is available as a keynote and 1 day workshop.

Through this powerful presentation, youth learn that regardless who you are, where you've been, the choices or mistakes you may have made in the past, what it looks like or what you feel like, IT IS POSSIBLE. It is possible to dream and to make your dreams a reality and it is possible to choose.

To Book Valerie Jeannis or to learn more about REAL Talk presentations contact us at Info@ValerieJeannis.com or 347-871-3246.

Valerie Jeannis

SOS – STATE OF EMERGENCY

Valerie created this special program in response to the needs of different community groups and schools that are facing challenges with their young women.

Over the past two decades, we have seen an influx of issues and challenges grow rampant among youth from bullying to suicide to recreational drug use to sexual experimentation to a spike in teen pregnancy. Some communities have been hit harder than others and are at a lost as to what to do, which is when Valerie is called to create an SOS – **State of Emergency Presentation Series**.

Valerie works in collaboratively with schools, communities and private organizations to create customized programs for that specific organization based on the issue(s) that they are currently facing.

Through multimedia, art, music, movement, discussions, writing, object lessons, theatre games, guest speakers and a variety of other dynamic and interactive activities, participants will be guided to develop the skills, tools and habits necessary to navigate the issues that are currently being faced.

These include:
1. Tools for self-reflection and discovery
2. An appreciation of her own multi-faceted giftedness and beauty (self-esteem)
3. Body knowledge and respect
4. Effective communication skills
5. Conflict Resolution/Bullying
6. Responsibility for her own decisions

I AM BEAUTIFUL

7. Awareness of her capacity to create her own path
8. Leadership skills
9. Development of networks and webs of support
10. Relationships - Friendships, Dating and Waiting

The objective is to:

- Provide relevant information
- Give them an opportunity to hear 1st hand accounts
- Answer questions that often go unanswered
- Motivate and equip them to make wise choices

If you are having an issue or crisis within your group or community then this may be the solution that you need. Send an email to Info@ValerieJeannis.com or call 347-871-3246 to set up an appointment.

* Due to the intensity of the preparation, Valerie only takes on a limited number of projects per year.

Valerie Jeannis

FREE MONTHLY TRAINING CALLS

GIRL Talk
Free training call for young women based on the questions that they submit.

With the right information we can equip out young women to make better choices.

So on the 1st Tuesday of every month, Valerie answers questions submitted by the young women.

It is a jam-packed 60 minute call with information delivered in a variety of fun ways including through guest speakers, poetry, drama, etc.

FREE Monthly Strategy Call for Parents and Educators
On the 1st Thursdays of every month Valerie tackles your biggest questions about dealing with young people in your life ... so that you can help them you can create the personal, professional and spiritual life they deserve. You can also use the same principles to create the life that *you* want and deserve.

I AM BEAUTIFUL

TRAINING PROGRAMS FOR YOUNG WOMEN

I Am Beautiful Academy

"It's like a modern day charm school and empowerment training in one powerful program helping young women discover who they are, learn how to put their best self forward, and define the life of their dreams. An absolute must for every young woman, whether she's coming of age, a teen or college bound."

I Am Beautiful Academy is a 15 week online training program that guides young women through a journey of self-discovery. This program gives young women of all ages the foundation needed to achieve success earlier in life.

Trainings are delivered through a series of online videos.

I Am a Super Role Model™ Leadership Program

If we want to train up young leaders, then we are going to have to give them opportunities to lead, which is exactly what they do over the course of this 9-week program.

The young leaders (our Super Role Models) will decide on a project of their choice based on an issue or topic that is important to them and over the course of the program they will be guided to complete their project through a series of creative lessons, guest speakers, training lessons and a variety of other methodologies that will enrich their learning experience.

Valerie Jeannis

I AM BEAUTIFUL

More Information

To book Valerie Jeannis or to learn more about REAL Talk Presentations
Please contact us at:

347-871-3246
Or send email to:
info@ValerieJeannis.com

Sign up for our newsletter and **FREE** monthly Training Call for Parents and Educators at
www.ValerieJeannis.com

Made in the USA
Charleston, SC
21 August 2012